ISSUES today

*A resource for **KS3***

Tourism

the last date stamped be...

Owen

ISSUE
20

Independence

Educational Publishers

Cambridge

First published by Independence

The Studio, High Green, Great Shelford

Cambridge CB22 5EG

England

© Independence 2008

British Library Cataloguing in Publication Data

Tourism – (Issues Today Series)

I. Owen, Claire II. Series

338.4'791

ISBN 978 1 86168 467 7

Acknowledgements

The publisher is grateful for permission to reproduce the
following material.

While every care has been taken to trace and acknowledge
copyright, the publisher tenders its apology for any accidental
infringement or where copyright has proved untraceable. The
publisher would be pleased to come to a suitable arrangement
in any such case with the rightful owner.

Chapter One: Tourism Trends

Trends in the travel industry for 2008, © ABTA, *Key UK tourism
facts*, © VistBritain, *Brits left cold by tourist hot spots*, © Virgin
Travel Insurance, *Rise in specialist holidays*, © TravelMole,
Travel trends, © Crown copyright is reproduced with the
permission of Her Majesty's Stationery Office, *Gap years – a
rough guide*, © The National Youth Agency, *Ditch (un)worthy
causes*, © VSO.

Chapter Two: Responsible Travel

Thoughts on tourism, © Different Travel, *Tourism and people*,
© Planet 21, *Insider guide: sustainable tourism*, © The Travel
Foundation, *Taking tourism to task*, © Economic and Social
Research Council, *Climate change and tourism*, © Thomson
Reuters, *Forget the carbon footprint, we want our summer sun*,
© Tiscali, *Nature's 'doom' is tourist boom*, © Telegraph Group
Ltd, *What is ecotourism?*, © i-to-i, *Souvenir alert*, © WWF-UK,
Murder, genocide and war: the new tourist attractions,
© Sunday Herald.

All illustrations, including the cover, are by Don Hatcher.

Design and production, on behalf of Independence,
by Hart McLeod Limited, Cambridge.

Printed in Great Britain by MWL Print Group Ltd.

Claire Owen

Cambridge

September, 2008

Tourism

T09667

338.491

Contents

Chapter One: Tourism Trends

Chapter Two: Responsible Travel

About Key Stage 3

Key Stage 3 refers to the first three years of secondary schooling, normally years 7, 8 and 9, during which pupils are aged between 11 and 14.

About Issues Today

Issues Today is a series of resource books on contemporary social issues for Key Stage 3 pupils. It is based on the concept behind the popular *Issues* series for 14- to 18-year-olds, also published by Independence.

Each volume contains information from a variety of sources, including government reports and statistics, newspaper and magazine articles, surveys and polls, academic research and literature from charities and lobby groups. The information has been tailored to an 11 to 14 age group; it has been rewritten and presented in a simple, straightforward format to be accessible to Key Stage 3 pupils.

In addition, each *Issues Today* title features handy tasks and assignments based on the information contained in the book, for use in class, for homework or as a revision aid.

Issues Today can be used as a learning resource in a variety of Key Stage 3 subjects, including English, Science, History, Geography, PSHE, Citizenship, Sex and Relationships Education and Religious Education.

About this book

Tourism is the twentieth volume in the *Issues Today* series. It looks at current tourist trends and the issues surrounding responsible travel. Tourism is a booming industry, with travel becoming more accessible and people taking more trips than ever. However, there are many concerns about the impact tourists are having on the environment and local communities they visit. What are the benefits and costs of tourism and how can we be responsible travellers?

Tourism offers a useful overview of the many issues involved in this topic. However, at the end of each article is a URL for the relevant organisation's website, which can be visited by pupils who want to carry out further research.

Because the information in this book is gathered from a number of different sources, pupils should think about the origin of the text and critically evaluate the information that is presented. Does the source have a particular bias or agenda? Are you being presented with facts or opinions? Do you agree with the writer?

At the end of each chapter there are two pages of activities relating to the articles and issues raised in that chapter. The 'Brainstorm' questions can be done as a group or individually after reading the articles. This should prompt some ideas and lead on to further activities. Some suggestions for such activities are given under the headings 'Oral', 'Moral Dilemmas', 'Research', 'Written' and 'Design' that follow the 'Brainstorm' questions.

For more information about *Issues Today* and its sister series, *Issues* (for pupils aged 14 to 18), please visit the Independence website.

www.independence.co.uk

Trends in the travel industry for 2008

NEARLY 70 MILLION VISITS abroad were taken by UK residents in 2007. The number of UK residents' visits to Europe have broadly stayed the same, with early bookings to Portugal and Turkey doing particularly well for 2008. Travel to the US has gone up this year about 3%, which will make 2007 the second best year ever for the States, but the quickest growth in travel is to other long haul destinations, which grew on average at about 10%.

Hot issues

Responsible tourism and climate change

The travel industry understands that, like every other industry sector, it has to take responsibility for its share of emissions. The most obvious way to do this is through carbon offsetting schemes, of which there are many including ABTA's own carbon reduction initiative – Reduce My Footprint – which encourages companies and individuals to avoid (non-essential activities), reduce (energy consumption), substitute (or switch to renewable sources of energy) and offset what remains. But emissions trading may well replace the need for offsetting schemes in the next few years. It is now also broadly understood that tourism can be damaging to destination environments and local communities and there are now many guidelines available and good practice examples to follow to make sure that tourism is a force for good.

Airport security and queues

Congestion clogs the workings of airports in the south east of Britain. Increased security has been partly to blame and early in 2008 some airports were allowed to relax some hand baggage restrictions. Terminal 5 in Heathrow opened in March relieving some of the pressure, but arguments will still continue about airport and runway expansion.

Mergers

'The big four', became 'the big two' in 2007 and the effects of having the two biggest tour operators in Europe based in the UK will be felt throughout 2008. Both have committed to continue to provide popular package holidays and expand their independent travel options.

Internet

User Generated Content with web 2.0 has taken up much of the online travel industry in 2007 and this is set to continue into 2008. The web has continued to provide travellers with seemingly unlimited choice. Consumers now expect to find everything they need on the net. With greater numbers of comparison sites, portals, online video information, travel blogs and online customer reviews, it's been increasingly important for travel companies to stand out from the crowd.

Trends in the travel industry for 2008

Cruising

Cruising is one of the fastest-growing and most successful sectors in the travel industry. Ocean cruising has experienced a larger than predicted growth in 2007 and the number of UK cruisers in 2008 is expected to reach 1.55 million – a 14% rise on 2007.

The sector drives up standards of customer service and new customers are impressed and surprised with the range of destinations – from Alaska to the Antarctic, the Caribbean to the Yangtze – and excursions, which can include adventures on a Harley Davidson, watching penguins, or a hike in the mountains.

Short breaks

The short breaks market has matured considerably, but new airline routes into Eastern Europe will open up the region further. Morocco, especially Marrakech, is becoming a popular short break destination as the cultural differences make for a great and adventurous city break.

Domestic short breaks

Travelling domestically for a short break is also increasingly attractive. With no long waits at the airport, unrivalled entertainment and culture and rising standards of accommodation and food a short break in Britain is very enjoyable. The historical city of York has been voted as our favourite British city this year, but it is far from alone in its historical heritage. Watch out for excitement around Liverpool as it is the European Capital of Culture in 2008.

Ferries

As a result of changes made within the ferry industry, there has been renewed growth and interest in taking ferries. Customers enjoy short check-in times, and the convenience and freedom of having their own car.

Tourist trends

Designer and luxury holidays

PriceWaterhouseCoopers reports that the luxury travel market has grown between 8 and 9% a year over the past few years and estimates that it is worth £5 billion in the UK. The absolute top end of premium travel continues to boom, particularly with the hire of private jets.

One of the top reasons clients buy luxury holidays is for special occasions – whether that's a wedding, honeymoon, anniversary or landmark birthday. Beaches for relaxation are the number one request for luxury seekers, but often clients are looking for something more exciting. Big sporting events have become popular along with luxury skiing, diving, sailing, golf and spa breaks. Holidays that are aspirational, exclusive and unknown are also increasingly being sought.

Mini glossary

long haul – a long distance journey

emissions – substances released into the atmosphere

congestion – over-crowding

merger – when two or more companies join together

aspirational – something that is desired or aimed for

www.abta.com

The above information is reprinted with kind permission from ABTA, the travel association. © ABTA

19 December 2007

Key UK tourism facts

Tourism is one of the largest industries in the UK, accounting for 2.9% of the UK economy and worth approximately £85.6 billion in 2006 made up of:

Spending by overseas residents (£ billion)

Visits to the UK: 16.0
Fares to UK carriers: 2.9

Spending by domestic tourists (£ billion)

Trips of 1+ nights: 21.0
Day trips: 44.8
Rent for second ownership: 1.0

UK domestic tourism

▶ In 2007 UK residents took:

- 53.7 million holidays of one night or more spending £11.5 billion

- 18.7 million overnight business trips spending £4.5 billion

- 47.8 million overnight trips to friends and relatives spending £4.8 billion

Employment

▶ Over 2 million jobs are sustained by tourism activity in the UK, either directly or indirectly

▶ There are an estimated 1.45 million jobs directly related to tourism activity in the UK, some 5% of all people in employment in the UK.

▶ Approximately 132,400 of these jobs are in self-employment.

Inbound tourism to the UK

▶ The 32.6 million overseas visitors who came in 2007 spent £16.0 billion in the UK. 2007 was the first year to see a decline in the number of inbound visitors to the UK and inbound visitor spending since 2001.

▶ Total visits for 2007 are 32.558 million visits, a 0.5% decrease compared with 2006, with a decrease of 0.3% in spending to £15.955 billion.

▶ In 2007 the UK ranked sixth in the international tourism earnings league behind the USA, Spain, France, Italy and China.

The top five overseas markets for the UK in 2007 were:

Country	Visits (000)
USA	3,587
Germany	3,385
France	3,323
Irish Republic	2,975
Spain	2,158

Country	Spend (£m)
USA	2,554
Germany	1,217
Irish Republic	969
France	865
Spain	848

www.tourismtrade.org.uk

The above information is reprinted with kind permission from VisitBritain.
© VisitBritain

Brits left cold by tourist hot spots

THE EIFFEL TOWER and Stonehenge are the tourist 'hotspots' that leave the most Brits cold, according to research by Virgin Travel Insurance that reveals the most disappointing sights at home and abroad.

The findings have been explained by travel expert Felice Hardy, who suggested reasons why Brits gave certain landmarks the thumbs down, and warned that visiting some of the world's most popular sightseeing spots was often more likely to leave us feeling stressed out and ripped-off, than inspired, thanks to pickpockets, endless crowds and expensive ticket prices.

Instead, Hardy reckons we should be using our imagination and heading off the beaten track to find the 'wow factor.'

'It's easy to be swayed by brochures that opt for the mainstream and focus on clichéd tourist sights around the world, but many of them are overcrowded and disappointing,' says Hardy.

'Pick carefully and don't always go for the obvious – natural phenomena are usually more exciting than the man-made, and can be wonderfully free of tourists.'

Mini glossary

clichéd – commonplace and unoriginal

natural phenomena – things created by nature rather than humans

Virgin Travel Insurance's ten most disappointing sights

Overseas

1. The Eiffel Tower
2. The Louvre (Mona Lisa)
3. Times Square
4. Las Ramblas, Spain
5. Statue of Liberty
6. Spanish Steps, Rome
7. The White House
8. The Pyramids, Egypt
9. The Brandenburg Gate
10. The Leaning Tower of Pisa

UK

1. Stonehenge
2. Angel of the North
3. Blackpool Tower
4. Land's End
5. Princess Diana Memorial Fountain
6. The London Eye
7. Brighton Pier
8. Buckingham Palace
9. White Cliffs of Dover
10. Big Ben

www.virginmoney.com

The above information is reprinted with kind permission from Virgin Travel Insurance.
© Virgin Travel Insurance

Virgin Travel Insurance's top ten must-see sights

Overseas

1. The Treasury – Petra, Jordan
2. The Grand Canal, Venice, Italy
3. The Masai Mara, Kenya
4. Sydney Harbour Bridge, Australia
5. Taroko Gorge, Taiwan
6. Kings Canyon, Northern Territory, Australia
7. Cappadocia caves, Turkey
8. Lake Titicaca, Peru and Bolivia
9. Cable Beach, Broome, Western Australia
10. Jungfraujoch, Switzerland

UK

1. Alnwick Castle, Northumberland
2. Carrick-a-Rede Rope Bridge, County Antrim
3. The Royal Crescent, Bath
4. Shakespeare's Globe Theatre, Southwark, London
5. The Backs, Cambridge
6. Holkham Bay, Norfolk
7. Lyme Regis and the Jurassic Coast
8. Tate St Ives
9. Isle of Skye, Scotland
10. The Eden Project

17 August 2007

Rise in specialist holidays

ONLINE BOOKINGS FOR special interest holidays are booming, according to a report by Travelzest. The report, in association with the Centre for Future Studies, reveals that from 2002 to 2006 holiday packages fell by 8.9% and this drop is set to continue.

Chris Mottershead, chief executive of Travelzest said:

" We're moving away from a mass market culture to one of unlimited choice.

'Through the internet, reaching small and specialist markets is now economical, an example being that about a quarter of Amazon's book sales come from titles outside their top 100,000 sellers.

'It's a similar story in the travel industry, with the biggest growth sectors being in specialist breaks such as activity, health and spa, nature and wildlife trips and escorted tours such as opera, cycling trips, dance, cooking or wine-tasting. "

Dr Frank Shaw, foresight director for the Centre of Future Studies, said:

" People are spending more money than ever before on life-enriching experiences, such as luxury 'small indulgences' and travel trends reflect this.

'We are seeing much more sophisticated and confident travellers who care about the world around them and want authentic travel experiences.

'Both men and women are putting a high emphasis on 'me time' and are looking to blend hobbies with their holidaymaking. That might mean arranging a trip to Verona and booking tickets to an opera at the same time. Travel companies need to be much more focused on individualism. "

16 May 2007, by Bev Fearis

www.travelmole.com

The top 10 'niche' travel markets tipped to grow over the next five years are:

1. *Learn-a-skill-in the-sun (eg cooking, surfing, painting, salsa dancing)*
2. *Inner self escapes (eg yoga, meditation, spa)*
3. *Hobbies abroad (eg art, gardens, cycling)*
4. *Festivals & Fiestas (dance, opera, food & wine)*
5. *Eco-lifestyle*
6. *Wildlife & nature tours*
7. *Sports tourism (following teams and playing sport)*
8. *The home-from-home hotel*
9. *Soft and extreme adventure*
10. *Nip/ Tuck tourism*

Mini glossary

mass market – designed to appeal to a large number of people

enriching – improving

indulgences – things that bring pleasure and enjoyment

niche – especially suited to certain individuals

Travel trends

THERE WERE A RECORD number of tourist and business visits (that is, visits for less than 12 months) both to and from the United Kingdom in 2006, according to a report published by the Office for National Statistics. Visits to the UK by overseas residents rose 9.2 per cent (to 32.7 million from 30.0 million in 2005) and UK residents' visits abroad rose 4.7 per cent (to 69.5 million from 66.4 million in 2005).

Visits to the UK by overseas residents

In 2006, the USA was the country with the most visits to the UK (3.9 million) followed by France, Germany, Irish Republic, Spain, Netherlands, Italy, Poland, Belgium and Australia.

Visits to the UK were fairly evenly split between three purposes: holiday, to visit friends or relatives, and business.

Seventy-one per cent of visits to the UK were from European residents, 15 per cent from North America and 14 per cent from 'other countries'.

North American residents spent most per day on visits to the UK: £82 compared with £53 by European residents and £56 by residents of 'other countries'. An average visit from a North American resident involved nearly double the spend of an average visit from a European.

Poland was the country with the biggest increase in the number of visits to the UK between 2002 and 2006 (0.2 million to 1.3 million, an increase of 1.1 million) followed by Spain (an increase of 1.0 million) Germany (0.9 million) and France (0.6 million).

The average length of stay per visit to the UK in 2006 was eight nights.

Almost a half of visits to the UK (15.6 million) involved an overnight stay in London. Edinburgh (1.3 million overnight visits), Manchester (0.9 million) and Birmingham (0.8 million) were the next most-visited cities.

Those from Europe grew most, notably from Poland, Spain, and Germany. Outside of Europe, the USA and Australia had the largest growth from 2002.

In 2006, the USA was the country with the most visits to the UK.

Travel trends

Visits abroad by UK residents

- In 2006 over one third of visits abroad were to Spain and France (14.4 million and 10.9 million respectively), but their proportion of the total number of visits is decreasing over time as other destinations become more popular. Visits to France fell by an average annual 2.7 per cent from 2002 to 2006 while visits to Greece, Mexico and Austria also declined over this period.

- In spite of a relatively low rate of growth in visits to Spain between 2002 and 2006, Spain had the largest absolute increase in visits (up by 1.9 million visits) followed by Poland (an increase of 1.1 million). Outside of Europe, India and Egypt had the strongest growth.

- Compared with visits to the UK, visits abroad were much more likely to be for holiday (almost two-thirds of trips abroad were for this purpose) and almost a half (49 per cent) were for duration of 4-13 nights.

- The average length of stay abroad in 2006 was ten nights.

- Seventy-nine per cent of visits abroad by UK residents were to Europe, although that proportion is down slightly compared with 2002.

- Forty-two per cent of holidays abroad by UK residents involved a package holiday.

- Forty per cent of holidays in Europe were package but as travellers to Europe increasingly turn to independent holidays the number has declined from 17.8 million in 2002 to 14.9 million in 2006.

Mode of travel

- Air was by far the most used mode of travel, accounting for 75 per cent of visits to the UK and 81 per cent of visits abroad. Trips made by air grew by 12 per cent to the UK and by 5.3 per cent for trips abroad between 2005 and 2006.

- There was a rise of 3.9 per cent in sea travel between 2005 and 2006 (although neither sea nor channel tunnel travel is growing strongly in the long term).

Figures released 23 January 2008

DID YOU KNOW? *Spending by UK residents abroad rose to £34.4 billion in 2006.*

Gap years – a rough guide

TAKING A YEAR OUT (or 'Gap Year') offers the chance to experience a different way of life, take a break from studying, make new friends, see new places and have an adventure. A gap year can be a time of education, fun and for young people to learn about themselves and the world.

Tony Higgins, Chief Executive of UCAS, says: 'UCAS believes that students who take a well-planned structured year out are more likely to be satisfied with, and complete, their chosen course. The benefits of a well-structured year out are now widely recognised by universities and colleges and cannot fail to stand you in good stead in later life.'

Gap year facts

Here are some gap year facts that may help you make the decision to stay or go:

- 200,000 young people take gap years each year.

- Australia is the number one destination.

- 'Gappers' can travel or work for 15 months between school and university.

- You don't have to go overseas – there are thousands of opportunities here in the UK.

- Universities are actively encouraging gap years. Students who have spent their time constructively are more confident and are more likely to choose a course that suits them.

- Don't let money put you off. Funding may be available from charitable trusts and foundations.

- Almost every 'Gapper' says their year out was the best thing they ever did.

- Only one in five young people who seriously consider taking a gap year go through with it.

What to do

There are hundreds of opportunities, and activities are vast and varied. Here are some suggestions for what to do, based on the most popular choices:

- ▶ Work for cash in hand: tread grapes in Australia, become a waiter in a ski resort.

- ▶ Go globe trotting: see the world before the hard work starts at college.

- ▶ Have an adventure or discovery holiday.

- ▶ Try a cultural exchange: be involved in another community, soak up their language and lifestyle.

- ▶ Become an eco-warrior: help survey endangered coral reefs or protect threatened environments.

Staying at home

If staying at home is the preferred option (perhaps you have retakes to sit or plans you've made with friends have fallen through) there are still plenty of opportunities. At home a 'Gapper' might:

- ▶ Learn a new language: this may stand you in good stead later both at work and in life.

- ▶ Try volunteering: you can stay close to home to do this if travelling far away doesn't appeal.

- ▶ Take on a teaching placement – either at home or abroad.

- ▶ Learn something that wasn't on offer at school: what about first aid, juggling or Tae Kwon-do?

Gap years – a rough guide

Making it different

The arrival of cheaper air travel means that fascinating faraway places are no longer as inaccessible as they once were. However, it can be useful to think beyond the obvious choices. Just because everyone else is 'doing Australia' or working at summer camp in America doesn't mean you have to. Superb gap year experiences can be found without even leaving the country – Britain is diverse and has much to offer.

Look for something that broadens your horizons. You could visit a new country, taking on voluntary work that will connect you with different communities and cultures. You could take on a job that teaches you new skills, or try something challenging. It doesn't have to be white water rafting or bungee jumping to be challenging!

Don't try to cram too much into a year out. You need time to appreciate the view along the way. It is beneficial to work out a carefully structured itinerary that takes rest days into account as an essential part of the travelling experience.

HOME

THE BIG WIDE WORLD

Mini glossary

UCAS – *Universities and Colleges Admissions Service; deals with applications for higher education in the UK*

itinerary – *a plan made for a journey*

www.youthinformation.com

Tips for making travelling safe

► Make sure you understand the culture and social issues of the country you are visiting. Seek out relevant resources (travel books, websites).

► Make sure you have appropriate clothing for the country you are visiting, both in terms of the climate and what is considered acceptable.

► Be wary of taking photographs – not all cultures welcome this.

► Don't get conned. Sometimes you just have to say 'no' and walk away. Many people living in poorer nations imagine Western travellers to possess fabulous wealth. If a situation makes you feel uncomfortable, don't take risks – just leave.

► You may not be able to learn a language, but at least learn a few basic phrases and don't be afraid to use them.

► Make sure someone back home knows where you are going. Leave someone a copy of your itinerary and phone/email home once a week.

► www.gapyear.com/gaplasses/ – a section of advice for women travelling the world.

► Don't count your money in public. Take travellers cheques where possible as they come with insurance if they are stolen.

► check if you can drink tap water or not before you do!

► http://www.fco.gov.uk/ – the website of the Foreign and Commonwealth Office includes information on travelling safety.

Ditch (un)worthy causes

INTERNATIONAL DEVELOPMENT CHARITY VSO is cautioning young people who are taking a gap year abroad that it may be better to travel rather than take up spurious voluntary work in developing countries.

The charity is concerned that young people are coming under increasing pressure to volunteer overseas during their gap year. While it encourages volunteering for people of all ages, it says that badly planned and supported 'voluntourism' schemes may be having a negative impact on young people and the communities they work with. It is advising young people who are serious about gap year voluntary work to carefully research who they go with and choose a development focused organisation.

Judith Brodie, Director of VSO UK said:

" Spending your gap year volunteering overseas has become a rite of passage for young people and the gap year market has grown considerably. While there are many good gap year providers we are increasingly concerned about the number of badly planned and supported schemes that are spurious – ultimately benefiting no one apart from the travel companies that organise them. Young people want to make a difference through volunteering, but they would be better off travelling and experiencing different cultures, rather than wasting time on projects that have no impact and can leave a big hole in their wallet. "

14 August 2007

Fact box

✔ The average gap year traveller spends around £4,800. (Mintel)

✔ The British gap year travel market comprises approximately 1% of all UK outbound trips and around 10% of outbound travel expenditure. (Mintel)

✔ Up to 200,000 Britons take a gap year every year, 130,000 of them are school-leavers. (Year Out Group)

Gap year checklist

If you're planning on heading overseas to volunteer ask the organisation you contact these questions before you decide:

1. Will you be given a defined role and purpose?

2. Will you meet face to face with your provider and attend a selection day to assess your suitability for the volunteering opportunities and gain detailed information about the structure of your placement?

3. How much will it cost and what does this pay for?

4. How will you be supported with training and personal development needs before, during and after your placement?

5. Is the work you do linked to long-term community partnerships that have a lasting impact? And how do volunteers work in partnership with the local community?

6. Does the organisation you are going with have established offices overseas that work in partnership with local people?

7. Can your organisation guarantee you 24 hour a day health, safety and security assistance?

8. Does the organisation have a commitment to diversity amongst its volunteers?

9. How does the organisation encourage long-term awareness of real development issues?

10. How will your work be monitored and evaluated so that others can build on what you have done?

Mini glossary

spurious – *not genuine*

rite of passage – *a traditional custom that marks a change in someone's life, like that from adolescence to adulthood*

www.vso.org.uk

The above information is reprinted with kind permission from Voluntary Service Overseas. © VSO

Activities

Brainstorm

Brainstorm to find out what you know about tourism.

1. What is tourism?

   ....

   ....

2. What are the main reasons people travel?

   ....

   ....

3. What is a gap year?

   ....

   ....

Oral activities

4. In a group come up with as many different types of holiday as you can think of.

   NOTES ....

   ....

5. With a partner, discuss the advantages and disadvantages of booking a package holiday against organising your own holiday. Which would you prefer?

   NOTES ....

   ....

Moral Dilemmas

6. You are planning a trip to France for a weekend. You could travel by ferry, but this would take three times as long as going by plane. However, your carbon footprint would be much smaller. You want to get to France quickly and enjoy as much of your weekend there as possible, but also care about the environment. Which method of travel do you choose?

7. You are planning your gap year and would like to do some volunteering abroad, but you have a limited budget. You have found a company you can afford to go away with, but you are sceptical about how much their work will really benefit the community. What do you do?

Activities

Research activities

8. Imagine you are planning a holiday with your family. Research the holiday online and compare all the options available to you. Look at where you would go, how you would travel, where you would stay and what activities you would do. Think about how the internet has changed the way people plan their holidays.

    NOTES..

    ....

    ....

    ....

9. Do a survey of your class to find out where everyone went on their last holiday. Are there any patterns? Show the results in a graph.

Written activities

10. Imagine you are going on an exchange trip with a student from another country. On a separate sheet write them a letter suggesting all the things you think they would enjoy doing in the UK during their visit.

11. Write a paragraph outlining the things you think have had the biggest impact on tourism in the UK in the last 10 years and how they have changed the industry.

    ....

    ....

    ....

    ....

    ....

    ....

    ....

    ....

Design activities

12. Design a poster that will encourage tourists to visit the area you live in, highlighting the main tourist attractions and activities they can enjoy.

Thoughts on tourism

THERE IS NO DOUBT that the economies of many impoverished areas of the world have come to benefit hugely from tourism – after all, it is one of the three biggest industries on the planet!

In South-East Asia and the Indian subcontinent, this is more and more noticeable, where regions once only visited by backpackers have undergone rapid development, with investment in the tourist infrastructure benefiting many people.

Tourism dependency

However, in some areas, whole communities have now become dependent upon tourism because farming and traditional industries have been abandoned in favour of more profitable tourism-linked activity. This means that when tourism declines, the economic sustainability of the whole community will also be undermined. This is why the impact of the December 2004 Tsunami was so devastating. When the tourists didn't come – tourism workers were left without an income.

Furthermore, tourism has also had an impact upon the social fabric and the culture of many communities. In some areas the clash between traditional cultures and those of western tourists is noticeable, often with the western culture proving stronger, and indigenous cultures weakened or even threatened with extinction. After all, we have the money!

> *When tourism declines, the economic sustainability of the whole community will also be undermined.*

Our responsibility to be responsible

It is only right that when we relatively wealthy tourists enjoy the benefits of tourism, we should do so responsibly, by making sure that:

▶ we are not contributing to the exploitation of either people or the environment

▶ we are participating in 'fair trade' practices which benefit those who work so hard to make our holidays so great

▶ we are contributing to the sustainable economic development of the communities who host us

▶ we are respectful towards and assist in the maintenance of indigenous cultures.

Air travel – blessing or curse?

Air travel contributes to high-level carbon dioxide emissions, a big cause of global warming, which will have a huge impact upon the environment within just a few decades if left unchecked.

Yet if governments decided to tax airline fuels to discourage air travel, it would be the developing countries dependent upon tourism which would be hit, and long-haul travel would again become just for the very wealthy – reducing the number of tourists able to visit the developing world.

Therefore, we suggest that we do something as individuals to counteract our environmental impact, by purchasing and planting a tree, which will pay back our carbon debt to future generations.

Mini glossary

impoverished – *poor*

indigenous – *originally found in the region or country*

counteract – *make up for*

www.different-travel.com

The above information is reprinted with kind permission from Different Travel. © Different Travel

Tourism and people

TOURISM IS SAID TO BE the world's largest employer. It plays a crucial role in world economics and has a significant impact on many people's lives – but this economic impact has been relatively little studied. It is also hard to measure less concrete impacts such as the effects of tourism on local cultures.

These impacts can be both positive and negative. For example, in many countries of the South, a culture of beach boys has developed which is in complete contrast to their own traditions and customs and this in turn creates conflict in their societies. On the positive side, tourism can encourage pride in local traditions and support local arts and crafts.

Tourism brings income to the local communities and supports employment. It can, however, also cause price rises, especially in land and food, which may be disproportionate to the earnings of the local people.

Displacement

Local communities are sometimes forced off their land for tourism development.

► Pastoralist groups such as the Maasai and Samburu in East Africa are amongst the worst cases of displacement from lands that they lived on for centuries, due to conservation and tourism policies which have favoured safari tourism above the needs of the local people.

► 2004 saw the forced displacement of hundreds of indigenous people from the inner states of India, in Chhattisgarh, due to government plans to bring tourism to the area through the development of a national park.

► 2004 also saw the tsunami which was the biggest natural disaster in modern history and deeply affected the lives and livelihoods of coastal communities in Asian countries. In India and Sri Lanka, people even now remain displaced from their land and livelihoods because of planned strategic developments mainly for tourism, from which they have been excluded.

► Statements by the Chinese government and estimates by the Centre on Housing Rights and Evictions show that 1.25 million people have already been displaced as a result of Olympic related urban development.

► In 2006, 1.5 million visitors travelled to Cambodia to see the Angkor Wat temples. There has been a boom in tourism in the country but at the cost of the local people with outside investors and developers taking over their land for tourism purposes.

Child labour

The International Labour Organisation estimates that between 13 and 19 million children under the age of 18 work in tourism. This amounts to between 10-15 per cent of the total worldwide tourism labour force.

Handicrafts

Handicrafts offer an important avenue for women, the poor and indigenous communities to earn income from tourism. In Lalibela, the main cultural site visited by 90% of the tourists in Ethiopia, craft sellers earn only 1% of tourist revenue. On the other hand, In Lao People's Democratic Republic, crafts generate around $1.8 million in semi-skilled and unskilled earnings per year.

Tourism and people

Economic dependence

Many countries are heavily dependent on the tourism sector to improve their economies but an overdependence on tourism for economic survival might actually put a terrible strain on the industry. In countries like Gambia, 30 per cent of the workforce depends directly or indirectly on tourism. In small island developing states, percentages can range from 83 per cent in the Maldives to 21 per cent in the Seychelles and 34 per cent in Jamaica. (UNEP report)

Tourism and gender

Globally, 46 per cent of the tourism workforce are women, compared to an average of 34-40 per cent for the world's workforce as a whole. On average, women working in tourism earn 79 per cent of what men earn, and work 89 per cent of the hours men work – i.e. they are paid less and are more likely to be part-time. Women are much less likely than men to be found in managerial positions and tend to be found in the hotel, catering and restaurant sectors.

Working conditions

According to the industry group World Travel and Tourism Council, the tourism industry is estimated to create 1 in every 12.8 jobs or 7.8 per cent of the total workforce. This percentage is expected to rise to 8.6 per cent by 2012 which would mean that tourism is also the world's largest employer, accounting for more than 255 million jobs, or 10.7 per cent of the global labour force.

▶ Research gathered in seven different popular destinations by the International Travel and Tourism Research team led by Tourism Concern confirm that concern for job security, low wages with an overdependence on tips and service charge, long hours and unpaid overtime are found across many destinations.

▶ Trekking porters in Nepal, a country which in the past has heavily relied on income generated from trekking, typically earn £2-3 a day. Porters die every year due to the effects of altitude and inadequate clothing.

Leakage

'Financial leakages in tourism occur when revenues arising from tourism-related economic activities in destination countries are not available for (re-) investment or consumption of goods and services in the same countries.' (Third World Resurgence) There are hidden costs to tourism which can have negative economic impacts on the destination country and often the poorer countries are least able to realise the positive effects of tourism. This is due to 'leakage'.

▶ According to UNEP a study of tourism 'leakage' in Thailand estimated that 70 per cent of all money spent by tourists ended up leaving Thailand (via foreign-owned tour operators, airlines, hotels, imported drinks and food, etc).

▶ According to research, most tourists to The Gambia are Europeans buying a package holiday but little of this directly reaches the poor. Between 20 and 35 per cent of the package goes to hoteliers and the rest to ground handlers, tour operators, airlines etc.

10 June 2008

Mini glossary

disproportionate – a different size to what might be expected

pastoralist – someone who raises livestock

indigenous – native to the region

urban – relating to a city

revenue – money received by a company for goods or services

www.peopleandplanet.net

The above information is reprinted with kind permission from peopleandplanet.net. © Planet 21

Insider guide: sustainable tourism

ANYONE WHO TAKES a holiday can make a positive difference when they travel. Sustainable travel isn't about specialist or 'eco' holidays, it's for every person who takes a holiday... and it can make a huge difference at favourite destinations.

> **By doing simple things, we can help ensure that we protect the environment.** "

It can help protect the natural environment, traditions and culture – the things that make holidays special. And it can improve the well-being of destination communities – making sure that local people benefit from tourism and are happy to give visitors a warm welcome.

All of which can give us an even better holiday experience. As well as helping to ensure there are great places for us all to visit – for generations to come!

> **Sustainable tourism is simply about making a positive difference to the people and environment of destinations we travel to.** "

Travel that makes a world of difference

With the increasing debate over climate change and the drive to reduce carbon emissions, sustainable tourism gives us an opportunity to make a positive difference when we travel. By doing simple things, we can help ensure that we protect the natural environment and offer maximum benefit to the communities who live in the places we all love to visit.

The Travel Foundation partners with UK travel companies in order to make tourism a force for good – minimising any negative effects on the environment and using income from tourism to help protect precious natural resources. We also encourage the industry to buy goods and services from the local area. This decreases the need for imports (and the many miles these can travel) and allows families living in destinations to earn a better living out of tourism.

What is sustainable tourism?

Sustainable tourism is simply about making a positive difference to the people and environment of destinations we travel to:

▶ Respecting local cultures and the natural environment

▶ Recognising that water and energy are precious resources that we need to use carefully

▶ Helping to protect endangered wildlife and preserve the natural and cultural heritage of the places we visit

▶ Protecting and improving favourite destinations for the future enjoyment of visitors and the people who live there

▶ Buying local – giving fair economic returns to local families

▶ Enjoying ourselves and taking responsibility for our actions.

Responsible, sustainable, green, eco, ethical tourism... all these terms mean pretty much the same thing – holidays that benefit the people and environment in destinations.

Insider guide: sustainable tourism

Just some of the people we've already been able to help...

Ana Lilia is helping to protect cenotes – underground rivers and pools that you can snorkel and dive in – and a precious source of water for visitors and local families. Protecting life and tourism in to the future... and offering visitors a truly unique experience of Mexico!

Orwin is making a better living for him and his family by selling fresh, local produce to hotels... and giving visitors the real taste of the Caribbean! This is reducing imports and helping the environment.

Kamala is learning lace making, to sell souvenirs to visitors in Sri Lanka. This is helping to rebuild her life after tsunami, keeping traditional skills alive and giving visitors the chance to buy real local crafts.

Maria is opening a café because of a new excursion taking visitors in to the heart of Cyprus – keeping life in the traditional villages... and giving visitors a whole new experience of an old favourite.

These stories are just the beginning. We are working with the UK travel industry to develop similar practices at destinations across the world. For example, Orwin's experience is helping us to encourage other tour operators and hotels to source local food for their customers. Developing the new excursion in Cyprus, where Maria has opened her café, has led to the development of a written guide to help travel companies create more sustainable excursions for their customers to enjoy.

What can holidaymakers do?

Just little things can make a big difference at destinations. For example:

▶ buying locally made souvenirs or crafts

▶ eating at local bars and cafes

▶ going out on excursions that use local guides and drivers

▶ getting around on public transport, bicycles or even walking when possible

▶ taking quick showers instead of baths

▶ asking not to have towels and sheets replaced on a daily basis

▶ not buying products made from endangered plants or wild animals (including hardwoods, corals, shells, starfish, ivory, fur, feathers, skins, horn, teeth, eggs, reptiles and turtles)

▶ consider compensating for the environmental impact of your flight. Ask your tour operator if they are part of any carbon offset scheme.

DID YOU KNOW ? *Tourism is part of the services sector of the economy, also know as the tertiary sector.*

www.thetravelfoundation.org.uk

Taking tourism to task

IS INTERNATIONAL TOURISM a tool for reducing global poverty or a source of greater inequality between rich and poor?

Professor David Hulme, Deputy Director of the ESRC Global Poverty Research Group (GPRG), says: 'Tourism can make a significant contribution to growth, but because the benefits are distributed very unequally it makes a relatively small impact on poverty.' He gives the example of an African safari. 'Currently only one cent in the dollar of the cost of that safari feeds through to the people who actually live and work on the game reserve.'

Tourism and the environment

According to Professor Kerry Turner, Director of the ESRC's Centre for Social and Economic Research on the Global Environment (CSERGE), unconstrained tourism development in or near sensitive environments can result in severe air and water pollution and waste disposal problems, and it may lead to the eventual loss of tourism itself. He points out: 'The end state is an environment that is not fit for residents' or tourists' needs.'

On a more positive note, however, he argues that ecotourism (tourism managed on sustainability lines) can provide sustainable livelihoods and conserve valuable habitats, such as tropical forests and wetlands, for a variety of species.

Travel

Even the environmental damage caused when tourists travel to their destinations could lessen in future, says Dr Daniel Osborn of the UK Energy Research Centre (UKERC). 'We can expect to see more biofuels becoming available in the next few years and these should help limit increases in the levels of carbon dioxide in the atmosphere. Such technological developments will help keep travel options open.'

However, issues still remain concerning the environmental impact of aeroplane vapour trails and the increase in the number of people flying. Nevertheless, UK residents can still enjoy the option of guilt-free tourism by taking their holidays closer to home. Dr Jeremy Phillipson, Assistant Director of the Rural Economy and Land Use Programme (RELU), points to the vital role tourism plays in the UK's rural economy.

'Tourism is often a key driver of rural development. We saw this most starkly in 2001 when foot-and-mouth disease led to a £3 billion loss to the sector,' he explains. 'Estimates suggest that in 2000 rural tourism attracted £14 billion and that its 25,000 or so businesses hosted 80 million visits and overnight stays from domestic visitors. Tourism has many linkages into other parts of the rural economy and, in many respects tourism and leisure can be seen to be key elements of the new rural economy.' So, perhaps some Scottish midges instead of foreign bugs this year?

23 June 2006, by Judith Oliver

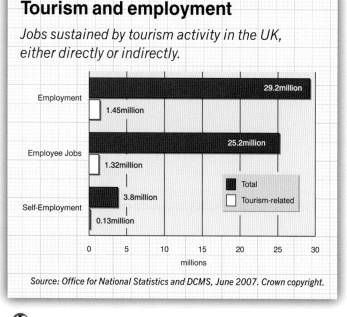

Tourism and employment

Jobs sustained by tourism activity in the UK, either directly or indirectly.

- Employment — 29.2million (Total); 1.45million (Tourism-related)
- Employee Jobs — 25.2million (Total); 1.32million (Tourism-related)
- Self-Employment — 3.8million (Total); 0.13million (Tourism-related)

(x-axis: millions, 0 to 30)

Legend: ■ Total   □ Tourism-related

Source: Office for National Statistics and DCMS, June 2007. Crown copyright.

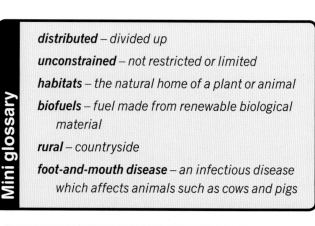

Mini glossary

distributed – divided up

unconstrained – not restricted or limited

habitats – the natural home of a plant or animal

biofuels – fuel made from renewable biological material

rural – countryside

foot-and-mouth disease – an infectious disease which affects animals such as cows and pigs

www.esrc.ac.uk

Climate change and tourism

TOURISM CHIEFS AND UN AGENCIES have pledged to 'green' the travel trade while highlighting the 880bn US$ industry's own vulnerability to global warming.

UN tourism, environment and weather agencies, national tourism officials and executives from 100 countries agreed the industry must 'rapidly respond to climate change' and take 'concrete measures' to cut down greenhouse gas emissions. They also said that tourists should be encouraged to consider the environmental impact of their travel choices and reduce their 'carbon footprint'.

'The immediate risk is that tourism is demonised for its carbon footprint and regulated because the industry doesn't act to regulate itself,' said Christopher Rodrigues, chairman of the VisitBritain tourism board.

Weather patterns

IPCC reports released earlier this year underlined that tropical cyclones, storm surges, temperature shifts, and changes in rain and snowfall are already harming tourism in some cases. The UN World Tourism Organisation has predicted that climate change would trigger 'very large' shifts in travel habits around the world.

In Davos, island states, beach holiday and winter destinations stressed their concerns about shifts in weather patterns, rising sea levels and declining snow cover that in some instances were eating away at their greatest economic asset. 'What's the main image used to promote a tourist destination? It's a nice landscape,' a UNWTO official pointed out.

The declaration underlined that new tourism policies must reflect a combination of environmental, climate change, social and economic needs.

3 October 2007

Carbon dioxide emissions

According to a UN report:

▶ *tourism accounts for up to 6% of global carbon dioxide emissions*

▶ *the number of travellers is due to more than double by 2020*

▶ *air transport currently accounts for about 40% of these industry emissions*

▶ *car travel accounts for 32%*

▶ *accommodation accounts for 21%.*

Andreas Fischlin, a leading scientist on the UN's International Panel on Climate Change (IPCC), told the meeting in Davos that 25 to 40% of all greenhouse gas emissions behind climate change needed to be cut by 2020.

The measures recommended by the conference included:

▶ *greater energy efficiency*

▶ *use of renewable energy*

▶ *better conservation of natural areas*

▶ *technological or design measures to avoid pollution*

▶ *staff education on climate change.*

www.thomsonreuters.com

Mini glossary

***demonised** – represented as evil*

Forget the carbon footprint, we want our summer sun

THE FIRST SUMMER LIFESTYLE REPORT conducted by broadband, telephone and media company Tiscali shows that Brits are far from concerned about their carbon footprint this summer. A massive 67% of Brits admitted that they won't even be thinking about the impact their summer holiday could have on the environment.

US, Australia and Maldives are Brits' dream destinations. The trend is only set to get worse. In 2007 we may be holidaying in Spain (24%), France (11%) or Greece (10%), but we aspire to long-haul destinations. 16% of respondents said their dream holiday would be to the USA, Australia (15%) and the Maldives (13%). The carbon footprint doesn't even register on the scale of our biggest holiday worries; what bothers us most is the possibility that our accommodation won't live up to scratch (28%) or that we might lose our luggage (26%).

What is clear is that we are chasing the sun in even greater numbers. 90% of us choose a more southerly destination, for a Brit sunshine inevitably meaning a flight to warmer climates. Only 4% would consider booking a holiday in the UK in the next 12 months, despite the fact that 54% of us remember childhood holidays in the UK.

Alex Hole, Tiscali's Online Media Director, says: 'A lot of people were brought up on day trips and summer holidays in Rhyl, Blackpool or Brighton – Britain's traditional summer resorts. But now lower flight costs and last-minute breaks are encouraging us to go for guaranteed sunshine and even exotic holidays. The government's new carbon calculator might get people checking out the carbon cost of their holiday but it's obviously not putting the Brits off their favourite sunny destinations.'

18 July 2007

www.tiscali.co.uk

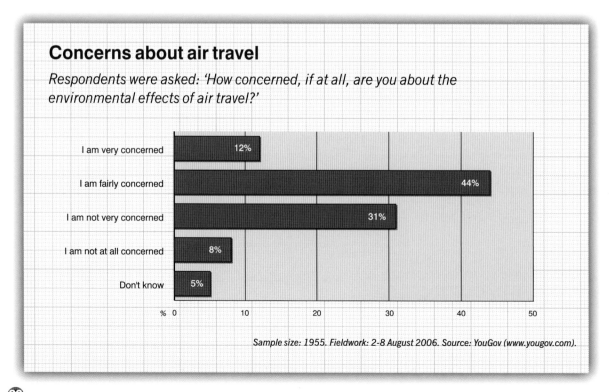

Concerns about air travel

Respondents were asked: 'How concerned, if at all, are you about the environmental effects of air travel?'

I am very concerned	12%
I am fairly concerned	44%
I am not very concerned	31%
I am not at all concerned	8%
Don't know	5%

Sample size: 1955. Fieldwork: 2-8 August 2006. Source: YouGov (www.yougov.com).

Nature's 'doom' is tourist boom

GLOBAL WARMING HAS LED to a new travel boom as holidaymakers embrace what tour operators are calling doomsday tourism – the urge to see some of the world's most endangered sites before they disappear for ever.

Newly awakened to the dangers facing the planet, American tourists are leading the charge to the melting glaciers of Alaska, Patagonia, the Arctic and Antarctic, the sinking islands of the Pacific and the fading glories of the Great Barrier Reef – and their British counterparts are not far behind.

Ken Shapiro, the editor of TravelAge West, a magazine for travel agents, said the phenomenon was one of the most significant trends in travel this year. He added: 'I called it the tourism of doom and I got a lot of responses from people in the travel industry.

'Many people are picking a holiday destination because it is threatened or endangered by environmental circumstances. We're hearing it from tour operators and travel agents.'

Rush to see the world

Some 10,000 tourists now climb Mt Kilimanjaro every year, where scientists say the peak snows could be gone within 15 years. The polar icecaps, which some scientists say are melting quickly, are also attracting record numbers of visitors. According to the International Association of Antarctic Tour Operators, more than 37,000 tourists visited the continent last year – double the number five years ago. 'There definitely is a rush to see and explore the world before it changes,' said Matt Kareus, of Natural Habitat, which operates excursions to Antarctica.

Quark Expeditions, a company that runs Arctic and Antarctic tours, is doubling its capacity and opening up new routes, including one to the Norwegian Arctic island of Spitsbergen.

Prisca Campbell, Quark's spokesman, said: 'There's not enough capacity to satisfy demand. We always get the question about global warming. There are many folks who are really concerned. Most of our American travellers look at the world and say, 'What's left?'?'

Damaging the environment

Critics say the rush to 'see it before it's gone' is speeding up damage to the environment, encouraging tourists to take flights and other means of travel that contribute to greenhouse gas emissions.

A spokesman for the Will Steger Foundation, a conservation group in Minnesota, said: 'It's hard to fault somebody who wants to see something before it disappears, but it's unfortunate that in their pursuit of doing that, they contribute to the problem.'

Miss Campbell said: 'Our philosophy is that you must protect the environment but you must make sure that people get to see it, because if you don't see it, you won't value it. People who travel to these areas are keen to help fight global warming. They go home and tell their friends they've got to do something.'

23 December 2007, by Tim Shipman

Mini glossary

phenomenon – *an occurrence that can be observed*

capacity – *the amount that can be produced*

What is ecotourism?

THERE IS NO UNIVERSAL DEFINITION for ecotourism, nor is there a certifying agency. A common misconception is that ecotourism is just nature based tourism, the act of surrounding yourself with nature's little wonders. The truth is far more complex.

Ecotourism has to be both ecologically and socially conscious. Its goal is to minimise the impact that tourism has on an area through cooperation and management and in some cases it even encourages travellers to have a positive impact on their new surroundings.

A commonly accepted definition of ecotourism is:

'Responsible travel to natural areas that conserves the environment and improves the well being of local people.' (The International Ecotourism Society, TIES)

Ideally, ecotourism should:

▶ Minimise the negative impacts of tourism

▶ Contribute to conservation efforts

▶ Employ locally and give money back to the community

▶ Educate visitors about the local environment and culture

▶ Cooperate with local people to manage natural areas

▶ Provide a positive experience for both visitor and host.

Eco-lodges

A hotel that is truly an 'eco-lodge' is one that makes efforts to conserve resources and limit waste. Some things a hotel can do to limit its environmental impact are:

▶ Reducing temperatures for laundry water

▶ Changing sheets and towels less frequently

▶ Using solar power or alternate energy sources

▶ Installing low flow showerheads and toilets

▶ Buying recycled products and recycling waste

▶ Building a compost heap or a waste treatment facility.

Greenwashing

With ecotourism being so popular, it is inevitable that many companies will claim to be environmentally friendly to get business. This is called greenwashing. Since there is no single certifying agency to determine who actually engages in ecotourism, it is easy to get away with just throwing the term around.

Many hotels claim to be eco-lodges simply because they have a good view. Wildlife viewing trips are often labelled eco-tours even if they give nothing back to local ecology and sometimes cause significant problems to the area's wildlife. Just because something is in nature doesn't make it ecotourism. It's important to look more carefully at their practices to see if it really is ecotourism.

DID YOU KNOW ?

According to the World Tourism Organisation, ecotourism is considered the fastest growing market in the tourism industry, with an annual growth rate of 5% worldwide.

Homestays

A popular alternative to eco-lodges is to stay in homestay accommodation. The main benefit of this is that your accommodation costs will be going straight back into the community. In many cases your meals are also included and this usually means that local suppliers will benefit from your stay too.

Many hotels claim to be eco-lodges simply because they have a good view. 99

Mini glossary

misconception – a mistaken belief

ecology – the relationships between living things and their environment

enhancing – improving

What is ecotourism?

Alternative tourism

Alternative tourism is any type of travel that is not mass tourism (i.e. beach vacations or traditional sightseeing tours). This includes ecotourism, backpacking, volunteer tourism, adventure tourism, historical tourism, tornado chasing, couch surfing or any other form of travel that is not typical.

Sustainable, alternative, responsible tourism – what does it all mean?

The terms ecotourism, sustainable tourism or responsible tourism are often used interchangeably. The main ideas behind these are all similar, but there are small differences.

Sustainable tourism

The widely accepted definition for sustainable tourism is 'Tourism that meets the needs of present tourists and host regions while protecting and enhancing opportunities for the future.'(The International Ecotourism Society, TIES) It has the same ideals as ecotourism but is not limited to natural areas.

Responsible tourism

Responsible travel is a practice used by travellers guiding how they act in a host country. It has roots in sustainable tourism but focuses on being respectful as a guest in a foreign country, such as asking permission to take photographs or enter a home, observing some of the customs, such as dress, or making an effort to learn the language.

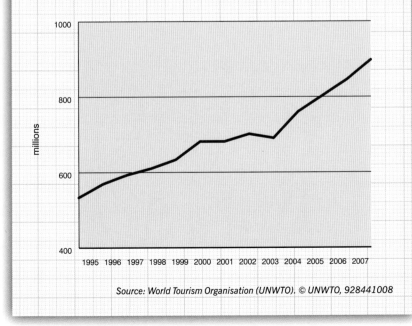

International tourist arrivals

World inbound tourism – international tourist arrivals.

Source: World Tourism Organisation (UNWTO). © UNWTO, 928441008

Souvenir alert

YOU MAY BE TEMPTED to buy wildlife souvenirs on holiday, but remember that trade in many animals, plants and products made from them is controlled internationally to protect wild species.

Almost 900 species of animals and plants are currently banned from international trade and a further 33,000 are strictly controlled by CITES (Convention of International Trade in Endangered Species) and European Union legislation. So think before you buy- you may be breaking the law and your souvenirs could be confiscated by customs on your return.

International trade in the following is banned altogether

It is not easy to know which souvenirs or gifts to avoid buying, so here's a brief guide to some you're most likely to come across. Your decisions can help these animals and plants to survive:

▶ Elephant ivory – watch out for stalls selling ivory carvings and jewellery outside hotels and shops, this occurs particularly in Africa and Asia

▶ Traditional Asian medicine containing endangered species – including species such as tiger, leopard, musk, rhino and bear

▶ Sea turtle shells – all jewellery, hair combs and sunglasses made from endangered sea turtles and often found in the Carribean and tropical beach resorts are banned

▶ Big cat furs – made from the skins and products of the jaguar, leopard, snow leopard, cheetah and tiger

▶ Shahtoosh – the wool of the endangered Tibetan Antelope which is used to make shawls.

International trade in the following requires a special permit

Trade in many plants and animals is controlled so that it does not threaten their survival in the wild. You may bring back souvenirs made from certain species where international trade is allowed, provided they are for your personal use and you have a CITES permit from the country of export:

▶ Live animals and birds

▶ Coral

▶ Queen conch shells

▶ Orchids and cacti

▶ Reptile skin products

▶ Caviar.

Remember, if you are unsure about whether you need a permit to import wildlife souvenirs from abroad, check with Animal Health's Wildlife Licensing and Registration Service before you buy.

www.wwf.org.uk

Murder, genocide and war: the new tourist attractions

TOURISTS ARE SHOWING an increasing appetite for death and disaster as increasing numbers flock to graveyards and killing fields around the world every year. From the modern-day fascination with Ground Zero in New York to the continuing pull of Auschwitz-Birkenau in Poland and even the Necropolis in Glasgow, 'dark tourism', as it is dubbed, is an industry on the up.

Professor John Lennon, of Glasgow Caledonian University, said the interest in our recent tragic past is showing little sign of decreasing. 'People want to go and be tourists in war zones while wars are happening. They seem to have an appetite to get very close while the blood is still dripping. There is no limit to the appetite for this stuff and demand is driving it faster and faster.

'We are always fascinated by the dark side of human nature and the most evil things people can do.'

Confronting the past

While around 700,000 people visit the Auschwitz death camps every year, new sites have been adopted by macabre tourists. Lennon notes how hundreds of tourists each day visit Ground Zero, 'trying to remember not to smile as they get their photo taken'.

Some countries, Lennon argues, are undertaking a worryingly selective approach when confronting their past, choosing only to address the glories and ignoring tragedy.

He added: 'In the Czech Republic, the Jewish holocaust is well covered but, by comparison, the genocide of the gypsy people, the Roma, is almost uncommunicated. That is a story that should be told, but people are not banging a gong for it.'

❝ For every ten that go to a site, there will be one that gets interested and learns from it. ❞

In Scotland, the two most recent tragedies – Lockerbie and Dunblane – were marked with gardens of remembrance and, while some people may prefer to destroy living memories of a tragedy, Lennon argues this isn't necessarily the best solution. He said: 'There is no limit to how low human curiosity can get, but it is a tough call to just destroy buildings. For every ten that go to a site, there will be one that gets interested and learns from it.'

Beyond the history book

A spokeswoman for VisitScotland said that though they do tap into the many ghosts and monsters that lurk around the country, this is as far as they go. She added: 'We would not brand this dark tourism as these are history-based themes and help raise and stimulate interest in Scotland.'

By 2008 more than 10,000 pupils from across the UK will visit Auschwitz as part of a nationwide educational project organised by the Holocaust Educational Trust (HET). HET chief executive Karen Pollock said: 'It is going beyond the history textbook. It makes them question further. It also allows them to shape the future by teaching young people to stand up and say something now, not wait till views, policies or actions have become entrenched.'

25 March 2007, by David Christie

www.sundayherald.com

Mini glossary

> **macabre** – gruesome; suggesting death or decay
>
> **holocaust** – the systematic killing of millions of Jews by the Nazis during World War II
>
> **genocide** – systematic killing of an entire group of people
>
> **entrenched** – firmly established

Activities

Brainstorm

Brainstorm to find out what you know about responsible travel.

1. What is sustainable tourism?

....

....

2. What is ecotourism?

....

....

3. What is tourism dependency?

....

....

Oral activities

4. With a partner, prepare and record an interview as if for radio in which one of you is the interviewer and the other an expert on climate change and tourism. Discuss the damage caused by air travel and what we can do to minimise it.

5. In a group, discuss the costs and benefits brought by tourism. Overall, do you think tourism is a good or a bad thing?

NOTES...

....

....

Moral Dilemmas

6. Imagine you have been travelling on a small budget and would like to buy some souvenirs to take home with you. You would like to buy some locally made souvenirs to put money back into the community, but they are more expensive than the souvenirs you could buy in the large shops in the area. Which souvenirs do you buy?

7. You have been looking forward to a family holiday abroad, but your parents are worried about their carbon footprint. They suggest having a holiday in the UK instead to help the environment, but say that the decision is up to you. Do you go ahead with your trip as planned, or are you happy to take your holiday in the UK?

Activities

Research activities

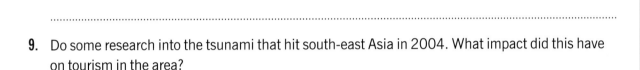

8. Look at the website, Tourism Concern at www.tourismconcern.org.uk. What are its main aims? What are their suggestions for how to be a responsible tourist?

    NOTES...

    ....

    ....

    ....

    ....

9. Do some research into the tsunami that hit south-east Asia in 2004. What impact did this have on tourism in the area?

    ....

    ....

    ....

    ....

    ....

Written activities

Complete the following activities in your exercise books or on a sheet of paper.

10. Imagine you are a businessperson opening a new hotel in a developing country. Write a brief business plan outlining the steps you will take to make sure your hotel is environmentally friendly and benefits the local community.

11. Write a letter to your MP telling them your concerns about tourism in developing countries and suggesting some measures you think we should take to improve the industry.

Design activities

12. Create an illustrated checklist for travellers to take on holiday with them, listing the ten most important things they should do to make sure they are a responsible tourist.

Key Facts

▶ Nearly 70 million visits abroad were taken by UK residents in 2007. (page 1)

▶ Over two million jobs are sustained by tourism activity in the UK, either directly or indirectly. (page 3)

▶ In 2007 the UK ranked sixth in the international tourism earnings league behind the USA, Spain, France, Italy and China. (page 3)

▶ Online bookings for special interest holidays are booming, according to a report by Travelzest. (page 5)

▶ There were a record number of tourist and business visits (that is, visits for less than 12 months) both to and from the United Kingdom in 2006, according to a report published by the Office for National Statistics. (page 6)

▶ 200,000 young people take gap years each year. (page 8)

▶ There is no doubt that the economies of many impoverished areas of the world have come to benefit hugely from tourism – after all, it is one of the three biggest industries on the planet. (page 13)

▶ Tourism brings income to local communities and supports employment. It can, however, also cause price rises, especially in land and food, which may be disproportionate to the earnings of the local people. (page 14)

▶ Unconstrained tourism development in or near sensitive environments can result in severe air and water pollution and waste disposal problems, and it may lead to the eventual loss of tourism itself. (page 18)

▶ According to a UN report tourism accounts for up to 6% of global carbon dioxide emissions and the number of travellers is due to more than double by 2020. (page 19)

▶ The first Summer Lifestyle Report conducted by Tiscali shows that Brits are far from concerned about their carbon footprint this summer. A massive 67% of Brits admitted that they won't even be thinking about the impact their summer holiday could have on the environment. (page 20)

▶ According to the International Association of Antarctic Tour Operators, more than 37,000 tourists visited the continent last year – double the number five years ago. (page 21)

▶ A commonly accepted definition of ecotourism is: 'Responsible travel to natural areas that conserves the environment and improves the well being of local people.' (page 22)

Glossary

Carbon footprint – Your carbon footprint is a calculation of the impact you have on the environment. It is based on the amount of greenhouse gases which are produced by your activities and measured in units of carbon dioxide.

Carbon offsetting – A way of compensating for your carbon dioxide emissions by contributing to an organisation who will either remove or prevent an equivalent amount of emissions elsewhere.

'Dark tourism' – A term used to describe the trend for visiting sites that are known for death, suffering and tragedy.

Domestic tourism – When people travel or take holidays within the country they live in.

'Doomsday tourism' – A term used to describe the new trend for visiting endangered areas, such as the polar icecaps, which are under environmental threat before they are damaged or even disappear forever.

Ecotourism – A form of responsible travel to a natural area, when the tourist is committed to conserving the environment and improving the lives of local people.

Endangered – At risk of disappearing or becoming extinct.

Exploitation – When people or resources are taken advantage of or used only for the benefit of other people.

Gap year – A period spent travelling, volunteering or working abroad, typically taken by students for a year between leaving secondary school and starting university, or between leaving university and starting work.

Heritage – Something to be preserved and passed on to future generations.

Mass tourism – Tourism undertaken by a large number of people.

Package holiday – A trip arranged by a travel agent, in which travel, accommodation and food are all pre-arranged and included in the price.

Sustainable tourism – Sustainable or responsible tourism minimises the negative impacts of tourism through an awareness of cultural expectations, respect for local customs, support of local businesses and protection of the environment for future generations.

Tourism – Tourism is generally defined as travel for the purposes of recreation or leisure for a period of less than a year. Tourism is one of the largest global industries and an important source of income for many countries, but there are also many ethical and environmental problems associated with it.

'Voluntourism' – The term 'voluntourism' or 'charity tourism' refers to the growing trend of combining a trip abroad with volunteer work.